Cherished Czech Recipes

Collected by Pat Martin

border and folk art by Marj Nejdl

Calligraphy by Esther Feske

Edited by Dorothy Papich Crum, Kathryn Chadima and Joan Liffring-Zug

Stocking Stuffers by Mail

All of our "stocking stuffer" little books are postpaid. You may mix titles. Costs are: one book $3.75; two $6.50; three $9.00. Each additional book only $3.00.

Cherished Czech Recipes
Dear Danish Recipes
Fine Finnish Foods
Fantastic Oatmeal Recipes

Great German Recipes
Norwegian Recipes
Splendid Swedish Recipes

The Czech Book: Recipes and Traditions, 6x9 inches, 60 pages, $5.25; 2 for $10.00; 3 for $13.50.

Czechoslovak Wit and Wisdom, 5 1/2x8 1/2 inches, 40 pages, $4.25; 2 for $7.50; 3 for $10.50.

Please send for complete price list. 1988 prices subject to change.

ISBN 0-941016-46-3
Copyright 1988 Penfield Press
Printed by Julin Printing Company

**Penfield Press
215 Brown Street
Iowa City, IA 52240-1358**

Contents

THE AUTHOR AND ARTISTS

Pat Martin carefully selected this collection of recipes to reflect the food traditions of Czech-Americans. Many of the recipes have not been published previously, and a special section reflects traditional Christmas favorites of pioneer Czech families. Pat served as the first coordinator of the Czech Village Association in Cedar Rapids, Iowa.

Marj Nejdl, whose charming border design graces the cover, is a noted Czech-American folk artist. She is widely recognized for her craft in egg decorating.

Esther Feske, noted graphic design artist, is a prize-winning calligrapher.

Finding the Czechoslovakians

People of Czechoslovakian descent are found throughout the United States, and you know they are there by the preservation of their rich heritage through sites, sounds and names: Bohemia, New York; New Prague, Minnesota; Prague, Oklahoma; Prague, Nebraska; or wherever you find a St. Wenceslaus, a Saint Ludmila, or a Saint John Nepomuk Church, you will find a congregation of Czechoslovak names. Or try community halls for Sokol, or other Czech organization meetings.

The sounds of music and celebration of freedom and pride of heritage are heard at the many Czech Festivals held throughout the country.

CZECH FESTIVALS

From New York City to Corpus Christi on the Gulf of Mexico, to the great Midwestern states, Czechs in America proudly celebrate their heritage as a free people with nostalgic emphasis on the folk traditions of the Old World. Festivals and heritage celebrations are held annually in: Birmingham, Elberta, Foley, Mobile and Silverhill, **Alabama**; Berwyn, **Illinois**; Cedar Rapids, **Iowa**; Wilson, **Kansas**; Deville, **Louisiana**; Kansas City, St. Louis and Sugar Creek, **Missouri**; Clarkson, David City, Fremont, Lincoln, Lodgepole, Omaha, Prague, Utica, Verdigre and Wilber, **Nebraska**; Holmdel, **New Jersey**; Cleveland and Metamora, **Ohio**; Yukon, **Oklahoma**; Johnston, **Pennsylvania**; Rapid City, Tabor, **South Dakota**; Corpus Christi, Ennis, Houston, Praha, Rosenburg, San Antonio and West, **Texas**; Seattle, **Washington**; Milwaukee, **Wisconsin**.

Czechoslovak Sites of Note

The Czech Village, Cedar Rapids, Iowa, has a museum and library with wonderful displays of costumes and crafts along with historical information. In the Village are a variety of shops, meat markets, bakeries and restaurants. Here one can tour a home restored to display typical Czech architectural decor of the 19th and early 20th centuries; another is located in Usher's Ferry Park, Cedar Rapids.

In Corpus Christi, Texas, there is a historically significant restored Czech home; another legacy of Czechoslovakian heritage.

The C.S.A. Fraternal Life Insurance Company in Berwyn, Illinois, has a Czechoslovakian Heritage Museum and Library that maintains vast amounts of archival information.

contd.

Sites contd.

In Spillville, Iowa there is the Bily Clock Museum where the clocks, hand-carved by Frank and Joseph Bily, brothers of Czechoslovakian descent, can be seen. The museum is located in the building where Antonin Dvořák lived while working on his *New World Symphony* and other compositions. Nearby is the beautiful Saint Wenceslaus Church where Dvořák played the organ.

In Phillips, Wisconsin there is a monument in memory of the World War II destruction of Lidice, Czechoslovakia.

If you look and listen, you will find a sprinkling of Czech bakeries, meat shops, restaurants and gift shops, or hear the sounds of a polka band at gathering places throughout the United States.

Flour-base Thickener (Omáčky)

An important element in European cooking is a mixture of butter or other fatty substance and flour cooked together for varying periods of time depending on whether white, blond, or brown thickener is desired for final use. Omáčky, also "roux" in the widely used French term, is the thickening element in soups, gravies, sauces and other dishes. The proportions are: equal amounts by tablespoons of flour and of butter or fat. *To prepare omáčky:* Melt butter in a saucepan. When butter is hot, add flour all at once and stir with a wooden spoon. Cook the resulting mixture over a low heat, stirring continuously. Continue to stir until the flour has been absorbed into the butter and the mixture no longer sticks to the side of the pan. This will take 2-3 minutes. Cook longer for darker mixture. *Note:* All liquids must be at a high temperature, i.e., boiling, before mixing in the thickener.

Garlic Soup

3 cloves garlic
   (onion for onion soup)
1/2 tsp. salt

1 1/4 cups boiling water
3 slices rye bread, toasted and
   buttered

With the back of a spoon mash garlic with the salt to form a paste. Pour boiling water over the paste and let stand a few minutes. Place slices of bread in serving bowls and pour soup over them.

Heart Soup

1 beef or pork heart,
   quartered
1 tsp. salt
1/2 cup flour

1/2 tsp. caraway seed
1 med.- sized onion, chopped
dash of pepper

Cover heart with water, add salt, pepper, caraway seed and onion, and bring to a boil. Simmer for about 1 1/2 hours or until fork comes out easily and heart is tender to touch. Remove heart and dice. Stir about 1 cup hot liquid with the flour, then add to the soup, stirring until thickened. Add diced heart and serve at once.

Mushroom and Barley Soup

1/2 lb. fresh mushrooms, sliced
1/2 cup diced onion
1/2 cup diced celery
1/2 cup diced carrot
2 Tbs. butter or margarine
1 Tbs. flour

3 cups chicken or beef broth
1/2 cup medium pearl barley
1 1/2 cups diced cooked chicken
   or beef
salt and pepper to taste

In a 3-quart saucepan, sauté mushrooms, onion, celery and carrot in butter over low heat, about 10 minutes, stirring often. Stir in flour, then broth. Add barley, cover and simmer until barley is cooked, about 1 hour. Add cooked diced meat, salt and pepper. If a creamier soup is desired, stir in about 1 cup milk. Reheat. Serves 4.

Mushroom Broth

6 cups chicken broth   sherry (about 4 ozs.)
1/2 lb. mushrooms, chopped

Skim fat from chicken broth. Add chopped mushrooms. Simmer for 30 minutes. Add sherry just before serving.

Cream of Potato and Onion Soup

1 quart cubed raw potatoes
3 large onions, sliced
1 stalk celery, finely chopped
2 Tbs. butter
3 Tbs. flour

1 13-oz. can evaporated milk,
    add water to make 1 qt.
1 Tbs. salt
pepper to taste
shredded cheddar cheese

Cook potatoes in a quart of water until well done. Drain and reserve liquid; mash potatoes, and set aside. In a medium-sized pan, sauté onions and celery in butter until lightly browned. Sprinkle flour into this mixture; stir until blended. Add reserved potato water slowly and cook until soup is thick. Mix potatoes with evaporated milk-water, then add to soup. Add seasonings and heat through. Serve topped with shredded cheese. Serves 4 to 6.

Potato Soup

3 Tbs. shortening
4 Tbs. flour
2 medium potatoes, cubed
1 medium onion, diced
2 cloves garlic, diced

1/4 cup pearl barley
1 quart water
1/2 cup dried mushrooms
salt and pepper to taste

Melt shortening and brown flour in a heavy iron skillet; cool and set aside. Cook potatoes, onion, garlic and pearl barley in 1 quart water until done. Add mushrooms and browned flour to boiling soup. Boil a few minutes longer. Serves 4.

Potato Soup with Mushrooms

4 large potatoes, cubed
1 cup sliced mushrooms
   (fresh or dried)
1/2 stalk celery
2 quarts water

1 1/2 tsp. salt
2 Tbs. butter
2 Tbs. flour

Place all ingredients (except butter and flour) into pot. Cook until potatoes are done. Remove and discard celery . Mash the potatoes into the soup liquid.

In separate pan, melt the butter and add flour, stirring until all the flour is absorbed into the butter. Cook until medium brown. Add to boiling soup for thickening. Serves 6.

Tomato Soup

16 oz. milk
1/2 tsp. baking soda
   (prevents curdling)

1 16-oz. can puréed
   tomatoes
salt and pepper to taste (if
   using fresh tomatoes)

Heat milk and 1/4 tsp. baking soda in a small saucepan. In a medium saucepan, heat tomatoes and 1/4 tsp. baking soda. When both liquids reach boiling point, pour together. Do not boil. Soup is ready to serve. Quick-cooking rice can be added to the soup if desired, or cooked vegetables such as carrots and celery.

Dill Gravy

2 cups water (1 cup may
   be beef broth)
2 Tbs. flour

1 cup sour cream
salt, dill and vinegar to taste

Bring water to a slow boil. Mix flour and sour cream; add slowly to boiling water. Stir and cook just until smooth. Add dill, vinegar and salt. Mix well and remove quickly from heat. Serve immediately since this tends to curdle if reheated.

Tomato Gravy

5 small tomatoes
1 cup beef broth or water
3 Tbs. sugar
1 tsp. cinnamon
1/4 tsp. ground cloves

1/4 tsp. allspice
1/2 tsp. salt
3 Tbs. butter
3 Tbs. flour

Peel tomatoes; cook and strain to remove seeds, or put through a blender to purée. Add broth, or water, and remaining ingredients, except flour and butter. Brown flour in butter to make a roux; add to the tomato mixture and stir until smooth.

Raised Yeast

Some guidelines to follow for "raising" yeast:

Let crumbled compressed yeast dissolve in warm water or warm pasteurized skim milk (80° or 90°) for about 5 minutes before combining with other ingredients.

Greater heat and more moisture are needed to activate granular dry yeast. Use more water, but decrease by that amount, liquid called for in recipe, unless specified otherwise. Water should be 105° to 115°. Sprinkle granular yeast on surface of the water to dissolve readily.

To substitute: Use 1 package or scant tablespoon of active dry yeast for 3/5-ounce cake compressed yeast.

Crescent Rolls

3/4 cup warm water
2 pkgs. dry yeast
1 tsp. sugar
1 cup hot water
1 egg
1/2 cup sugar

2 tsp. salt
3 Tbs. butter
5 1/4 cups flour
1 egg, beaten with1 1/2 Tbs.
  water
poppy seed, caraway
  seed, or salt

Dissolve 1 tsp. sugar and yeast in 3/4 cup warm water. Combine egg, 1/2 cup sugar, salt, butter and hot water in large mixing bowl. Add 3 1/2 cups flour. Cool flour mixture to lukewarm, then add yeast mixture. Gradually add remaining flour until all ingredients are well-blended.

contd.

Knead for 10 minutes. Cover with a damp cloth and let rise in greased bowl until double. Cut 1 Tbs. dough for each roll and form into a crescent shape. Place on well-greased cookie sheets. Brush tops with the beaten egg and water mixture. Sprinkle with poppy seeds, caraway, or salt to taste. Cover and let rise until doubled. Bake in preheated 375° oven for 15-20 minutes.

Bohemian Rye Bread

1/2 cup water, lukewarm
1 small cake yeast
1 tsp. sugar
6 cups rye flour
1 Tbs. caraway seed

2 cups warm water, or potato
  water
2 Tbs. melted lard
1 cup white flour
1 Tbs. salt

Combine yeast, sugar and 1/2 cup lukewarm water. Allow to set in warm place for 5 minutes. Add additional 2 cups warm water, or potato water, 3 cups rye flour, melted shortening and caraway seed. Mix well; cover with waxed paper and let rise in warm place for 2 hours, until bubbly on the top.

Combine remaining 3 cups rye flour and white flour. Add mixture and salt to dough. Mix well, then knead on floured bread board until dough is

contd.

not sticky. Knead in more flour as necessary. Shape into large ball and place in greased, lightly floured bowl. Cover with waxed paper or cloth and let rise about 1 3/4 hours until light and doubled in size.

Turn onto board and knead until there are no bubbles. Form into 1 round or 2 long loaves and place on floured baking pan. Brush top with melted butter or margarine and pierce in several places with fork. Let rise about 1/2 hour. Bake at 350° (preheated oven) for about 1 hour, or until light golden brown. When finished baking, brush with water for a hard crust, or with melted butter or margarine for a soft crust.

Favorite Rye Bread

1 1/2 cups potato water, lukewarm
2 1/2 cups water, lukewarm
2 cakes yeast
2 1/2 tsp. sugar
1/2 cup mashed potatoes
2 eggs

2 Tbs. lard
1 Tbs. salt
1 cup rye flour
1/2 cup graham flour
7 cups all-purpose white flour

In a very large bowl, dissolve yeast with water and sugar. Combine all ingredients. Knead well. Cover with cloth and let rise in warm place until double in size. Punch down and let rise again until double. Shape into loaves and place in greased loaf pans; cover and let rise until double. Bake in preheated 350° oven for 45 minutes. (Freezes well after cooled.)

Honeybread

1/2 cup water

1 cup sugar

1 Tbs. honey

1 egg

1 tsp. baking soda

4 to 5 cups rye flour

Boil water, sugar and honey together for 5 minutes. When cool, add baking soda and egg; mix well. Put rye flour on a board; add liquid mixture slowly and work into a dough. Bake in greased loaf pans at 350° for about 40 minutes.

Old-Fashioned White Bread
(with doughmaker)

5 to 6 cups all-purpose flour
2 1/4 cups milk (or 2 1/4 cups
    water and 2/3 cups dry milk)
2 pkg. dry yeast

3 Tbs. butter
2 Tbs. sugar
2 tsp. salt

Heat milk and butter to 120°. In large mixing bowl, combine 3 cups of flour with yeast, sugar, salt and warm milk. Using dough hooks, mix for 3-4 minutes (to activate yeast). Gradually add remaining flour to form a stiff dough. Knead with dough hooks until dough is smooth and satiny, about 4-5 minutes. Continue to knead until dough no longer sticks to fingers.

contd.

Place dough in greased bowl, turning to grease top. Cover and let rise until double in size, about 1 hour. Punch down and shape into 2 smooth balls; cover and let rest about 10 minutes. Shape into loaves and place in 2 greased 9x5x3-inch pans. Let rise until double, about 45 minutes. Bake in preheated 375° oven for 10 minutes. Reduce heat to 350° and continue to bake 35 minutes. Remove from pans and cool on rack.

Variations:

Garlic Cheese Bread: Add 1 cup shredded cheddar cheese and 1 tsp. garlic powder during first mixing.

Raisin Cinnamon Bread: Add 1 1/2 cups raisins and 2 tsp. cinnamon during first mixing.

Onion Bread: Omit salt, and add 1 pkg. dry onion soup mix during first mixing.

Light Rye Bread: Replace 2 cups white flour with 2 cups rye flour and add 1 Tbs. caraway seed.

Marinated Beef

11 to 12 lb. piece of lean, top
   round of beef
salt
8 bacon strips, cut for larding
4 to 5 carrots, chopped
6 to 7 ribs of celery, chopped
1 onion, chopped
4 to 5 bay leaves
12 to 15 peppercorns

1/4 tsp. thyme
1/4 tsp. allspice
1 cup water
4 Tbs. vinegar
1/4 lb. butter, melted
cornstarch
1 pt., or more, sour cream
pinch of sugar
2 to 3 Tbs. lemon juice

Rub beef with a little salt. To lard, make several cuts in beef with point of a sharp knife and push a strip of bacon into each cut. Mix chopped

contd.

vegetables, spices, water, vinegar and melted butter. Cover meat with this mixture; put into a turkey-sized roasting bag, or stoneware crock, and refrigerate for 2 days. Turn meat occasionally during this period.

To roast, preheat oven to 350°. Place meat, vegetables and juices in roasting pan; if using a roasting bag, tie end shut, and cut about 6 small slits at top of bag for steam to escape. Bake for 3 hours.

Remove from oven and let cool a while, then remove meat from liquid and let cool further before carefully cutting into slices a little more than 1/4 inch thick. Press sauce from roasting pan through a sieve. Mix small amount of cornstarch and water and add to sauce (about 1 Tbs. to 1 cup of sauce). Simmer sauce until thickened, then add sour cream, sugar, lemon juice and salt to taste. Pour over the sliced beef. Serve with dumplings.

Bohemian Beef Dinner

1 tsp. salt	1 tsp. dill weed
1/4 tsp. pepper	1 tsp. caraway seed
1 cup flour (for dredging)	1 tsp. paprika
2 lbs. stewing beef, cubed	1/2 cup water
2 Tbs. oil	1 cup sour cream
2 medium onions, chopped	1 27-oz. can sauerkraut
1 clove garlic, minced	paprika for top

Mix flour, salt and pepper. Dredge beef in mixture and brown in hot oil. Pour off drippings. Add onion, garlic, dill weed, caraway seed, paprika and water to the meat. Cover loosely and cook slowly for 2 hours until meat is tender. Stir in sour cream and heat through, but do not boil. Heat sauerkraut in a saucepan, drain and place on a platter. Serve meat mixture over sauerkraut. Sprinkle with paprika. Serves 6 to 8.

Steak and Dumplings

2 lbs. round steak, cut into
   serving pieces
garlic salt
black pepper
3 Tbs. margarine
1/2 cup chopped onion

1 15-oz. can stewed tomatoes
1 8-oz. can tomato sauce
1 6-oz. can tomato paste
water
dumplings (prepared from
   favorite recipe)

Sprinkle pieces of steak with garlic salt and black pepper. Brown in skillet with margarine. Transfer browned steak to a kettle or Dutch oven; add chopped onion. Pour stewed tomatoes and tomato sauce over meat. Cover and simmer for 1 1/2-2 hours, until meat is very tender. Remove meat from sauce; place on platter and keep warm in oven on low heat. *contd.*

Prepare dumplings and set aside.

To meat juices in the kettle, add tomato paste and enough water to boil dumplings. Stir and bring mixture to a boil. Drop dumplings by tablespoonfuls into boiling liquid and cook uncovered for 8-10 minutes over medium heat. Turn dumplings gently with a spoon; cover and cook an additional 5-8 minutes. Serve with the steak. Serves 6.

Fried-Down Pork

pork chops, boneless, cut to 1 1/2- inch thickness
canning salt
lard (original recipe calls for "freshly rendered")

Rub each pork chop, both sides, with canning salt and place in large roasting pan. Bake in preheated 325-350° oven until brown; turn and continue roasting until golden brown, about 1 hour or more each side. After roasting, place chops in 3-gallon crocks, about 3/4 full. Pour hot lard over chops (make sure to pour between layers) to within 1 inch of top of container. Cover and store in cool dry place. These will keep for several months. To serve, warm slowly in oven and serve with sauerkraut and potato dumplings.

Goulash

2 lbs. pork, cubed
   (pork cheeks are excellent)
2 lbs. beef, cubed
2 Tbs. margarine or lard
2 large onions, chopped
1 cup chopped celery
flour or cornstarch

1 Tbs. salt
1/4 tsp. red pepper
1/2 tsp. black pepper
1 Tbs. paprika
1/2 cup catsup
2 or 3 peppercorns
1 bay leaf

Sauté onion and celery in margarine, or lard, until golden. Add meat and brown. Add enough water to cover; simmer covered until tender (about 45 minutes). Add spices and thicken gravy with a little flour or cornstarch mixed with cold water. Simmer for a few minutes, until flavorings are blended.

Hash

1 pig snout
1 cup farina
2 potatoes, boiled and mashed

water from potatoes
1 clove garlic, minced
salt

Boil pig snout in enough water to cover until cooked. Reserve cooking water. Grind the snout, then add cooking water, farina, mashed potatoes, potato water, garlic and salt. Stir well and put into shallow pan (a pie pan is good). Bake at 350° until brown.

Jellied Pork

Huspenina in Czechoslovakian, sometimes called *sulc*, the German word for the same dish.

2 or 3 lbs. pork skins	Marinade:
1 pork heart	2 1/2 qts. vinegar
1 pork tongue	2 1/2 qts. broth from cooked pork
2 lbs. pork trimmings, roast, or	2 Tbs. salt
8 pig tails	3 bay leaves

Cover pork with boiling water and cook until tender. If using tails, cook separately because of small bones. Reserve broth. After cooking, cut skins into 3- to 4-inch lengths. If using, debone tails. Dice rest of meat into 1-inch cubes. *contd.*

Stir together all ingredients for marinade and bring to a boil; add meat and bring to boil again. Pour into 6 to 8 loaf pans, 1 to 1 1/2 qt. capacity. Refrigerate until firm. Will keep 2 to 3 weeks refrigerated. To serve, cut thick slices for a meat dish, thin slices for sandwiches.

If you want to preserve longer, pour, while still boiling hot, into hot sterilized jars and seal. Can be reheated (add more vinegar if necessary), poured into a loaf pan and chilled.

Pork Cheeks with Sauerkraut

1 onion, chopped
2 lbs. pork cheeks
3 Tbs. butter
water to cover

sauerkraut
1 medium-sized potato, grated
salt to taste

Sauté onion and pork cheeks in butter. Add water and simmer until nearly tender. Add sauerkraut and continue cooking until meat is tender and well-done. Add grated potato and cook an additional 10 minutes.

Black Barley Dish

- 1 cup barley grits
- 2 cups water
- 1 lb. pork sausage
- 1 large onion, chopped
- 1 cup diced celery

- 2 cups mushrooms (or more) sliced, or chopped
- salt, pepper, sage, marjoram and garlic (caraway seed can be used in place of marjoram and sage)

Boil grits in 2 cups water until tender and most of water is absorbed. In a skillet, brown meat, onion and celery until tender. Add grits and mushrooms. Add seasonings to taste. Place mixture in a medium-sized flat baking dish and bake at 350° for 1 hour.

Baked Ham and Noodles

2 cups cubed or ground cooked ham
8 oz. medium-sized noodles
2 cups milk

3 large eggs
1/4 tsp. ground mace
salt and pepper to taste

Cook noodles in salted, boiling water until just tender (do not overcook). Drain well. Beat milk and eggs together. Combine noodles, ham, milk and egg mixture and seasonings. Pour into greased casserole dish and bake at 350° for about 1 hour, or until center is set. Serves 6.

Ham, Cabbage and Noodle Casserole

3 Tbs. butter
1/2 medium-sized head of cabbage, diced
1 8 oz. pkg. noodles
2 1/2 cups ground ham

2 1/2 to 3 cups milk
3 eggs, well-beaten
1/2 tsp. salt
pepper to taste

Cook noodles according to directions, until barely tender. Drain and set aside. Melt butter in a skillet and sauté cabbage until tender. In a buttered casserole dish, place a layer of half the noodles and a layer of half the cabbage. Add one layer of all the ham. Add the rest of the cabbage and noodles layered on top. Scald the milk and add slowly to the beaten eggs, beating constantly. Salt and pepper to taste and beat well. Pour over layered ingredients and bake at 350° for about 1 hour, or until a knife inserted in middle comes out clean.

Mushroom and Veal Loaf

2 lbs. veal
1/4 lb. veal fat
1/2 lb. pork
lean bacon

1 cup sliced mushrooms
cooking oil
2 eggs, slightly beaten
salt and pepper
1 to 2 Tbs. dry bread crumbs

Put veal, veal fat and pork through a meat grinder. To the ground meats, add the sliced mushrooms which have been lightly sautéed in small amount of oil, then mix in eggs, salt and pepper. If this mixture seems too soft, add 1 or 2 Tbs. bread crumbs. Shape into a long loaf and put into a baking dish. Place several slices of lean bacon under and on the top of the loaf. Bake at 350° for 1 hour. May be served hot or cold.

Chicken Paprika

1 stewing chicken (about 4 lbs.)
1 medium onion, chopped
1/4 cup butter
1/2 tsp. paprika
salt to taste

dash cayenne pepper
1 1/2 cups water (or broth)
1/2 cup sour cream
2 Tbs. flour

Cut chicken into serving pieces. Sauté onion in butter; add paprika, salt, cayenne pepper and chicken. Brown chicken, then add water or chicken broth. Cover and simmer until chicken is tender, 45 minutes to 1 hour. Remove chicken and place on a serving platter. Into hot, but not boiling, liquid mix sour cream and flour; stir carefully. (Do not boil; boiling tends to cause the cream to curdle.) Simmer for 5 minutes. Pour gravy over chicken. Serves 4 to 5. Dumplings go well with this.

Roast Goose or Duck

1 duck or goose
1 or 2 cloves garlic
salt

dressing, 3/4 cup per lb. of
   fowl (optional)

Clean, wash and dry goose or duck. Rub inside and outside of bird with minced garlic and salt. (Garlic salt may be used but use less of the regular salt.) Stuff lightly with choice of dressing, or leave unstuffed. (Czech cooks usually leave bird unstuffed and prepare dressing in another pan.) Place on rack, breast side up, in uncovered roasting pan. Roast at 325° for 40-45 minutes per lb. for duck; 25-30 minutes per lb. for goose. Pour off fat during roasting. Test for doneness by moving drumstick; if it separates easily from the body at the joint, the bird is done. If it browns too fast, cover loosely with foil allowing steam to escape. A crisp, brown skin is desired. A 4 to 5- lb. duck serves 4; an 8- lb. goose serves 5 to 6.

Fish in Sweet, Dark Gravy

fish, fresh or frozen, uncooked
1/2 cup raisins
1/2 cup pitted prunes

apples and peaches, dried
gingersnaps (crushed) or flour

Boil fruits with water to cover (pinch of salt added) until fruit softens. Add fish to the fruit mixture and cook until fish is tender. Remove fish when done, and thicken fruit mixture with gingersnaps, or flour. Return fish to gravy. May be served hot or cold; flavor is often better when allowed to set. Can be frozen and reheated.

Bass with Mushrooms

1 bass, about 3 lbs.
1 oz. cooking oil
paprika
salt

1 1/2 cups tomato sauce
1/2 lb. mushrooms, sliced
1/4 cup dry white wine

Wash and dry bass well. Fry bass in oil for a few minutes. Mix paprika, salt, tomato sauce, mushrooms and wine. Pour this mixture over the bass and bake in a moderate 350° oven for about 30 minutes.

Sole with Mushrooms

(Number of fillets will determine amounts of ingredients.)

sole fillets, fresh or frozen
salt and pepper
lemon juice

mushrooms, finely chopped
parsley, minced
butter or margarine
dry white wine with dash of water

Place sole fillets in a greased shallow baking dish; season with salt, pepper and some lemon juice. Cover the sole with chopped mushrooms, adding minced parsley and dabs of butter or margarine. Pour wine mixed with a little water around the fish, enough to steam but not to cover. Bake at 350° for 30 minutes. Add more wine-water if needed during baking.

Mushroom Salad

large mushrooms, about 1 doz.   lettuce
cooking oil, or butter   French dressing (optional)
1/4 lb. boiled ham, minced   fresh horseradish (optional)

Sauté mushrooms in oil, or butter, until lightly cooked. Remove stems and chop finely; mix with minced boiled ham. Fill mushroom caps with this mixture and place on a bed of lettuce. Pour a little French dressing (or choice) over each, and grate a little fresh horseradish on top (optional).

Cabbage Salad

6 cups shredded cabbage
1 cup finely sliced carrot
1/4 cup sugar
1/2 tsp. salt
1/4 tsp. pepper
1/2 cup milk

1 cup mayonnaise
1/2 cup buttermilk
1/2 tsp. celery seed
3 Tbs. minced dry onion
2 or 3 drops Tabasco sauce

Stir together cabbage, carrot, sugar, salt, pepper, and milk. Cover and refrigerate for 15 minutes. Combine mayonnaise, buttermilk, celery seed, dry onion, and Tabasco sauce. Pour over cabbage mixture and refrigerate at least 1 hour before serving. Makes about 2 quarts.

Wild Rice Casserole

1 cup wild rice, soaked
   overnight in cold water
2 cups fresh mushrooms,
   sliced
1/2 cup butter or margarine
2 Tbs. flour
2/3 cup milk

1 bay leaf
1 onion, sliced
salt and pepper
thyme
nutmeg
1/2 cup buttered bread crumbs

Drain soaked rice. Cover with boiling salted water and let stand 20 minutes. Drain again and set aside.

In a skillet, brown mushrooms in butter. Sprinkle with flour and blend well. Scald milk with bay leaf and onion. Strain and add to mushroom

contd.

mixture. Stir constantly until thickened. Add drained rice and season to taste with salt, pepper, nutmeg and a pinch of powdered thyme. Transfer to a generously buttered casserole dish. Sprinkle top with buttered bread crumbs and bake at 350° for 15-20 minutes.

Dumplings

2 cups water
3 cups potato flakes
1/2 cup grits

1 tsp. salt
2 Tbs. butter
2 eggs

Mix water, potato flakes, grits, salt, butter and eggs in a large bowl until smooth. Bring additional water to boil in large kettle. Divide and shape mixture into small balls. Drop into boiling water. Cover and boil for 15 minutes. Drain and serve.

Fruit Dumplings

1 1/2 cups flour
2 rounded tsp. baking powder
3/4 tsp. salt
2 eggs
milk

fruit (halved, pitted blue plums,
   fresh, sliced peaches)
melted butter
flour and sugar for center

Sift flour, salt and baking powder together. Add unbeaten eggs to a "well" in flour. Stir, adding just enough milk to make a medium-stiff dough. Place dough on floured board; knead lightly 2 or 3 times. Divide into 4 portions and roll each into 5- to 6-inch rounds. Spread 1/2 tsp. flour and 1/2 tsp. sugar on center of each round; place fruit on this mixture. Moisten edges of round with milk or water; bring edges together to close completely. *contd.*

Drop dumplings into a large kettle of boiling water and boil 15 minutes, turning once, until done. Lift dumplings carefully onto a platter; brush with melted butter. Flavor may be enhanced by cooking some of the fruit to make a thin syrup to pour over dumplings.

Liver Dumplings

1 lb. liver, ground (chicken livers
   excellent)
1 small onion, grated or finely diced
1 clove garlic, minced
1 cup bread crumbs
2 eggs

1 Tbs. chopped parsley
pinch of cloves
pinch of marjoram
salt and pepper to taste
soup stock, boiling

Mix all ingredients thoroughly, except soup stock. Drop by tablespoonfuls into boiling soup stock. Cook about 10 minutes.

Potato Dumplings

3 1/2 to 4 lbs. potatoes, boiled   2 cups flour
   in skins, peeled and mashed   1 Tbs. salt
2 eggs

Mix eggs, flour and salt with mashed potatoes. If potatoes are very moist, use more flour as needed. Place dough on a floured board; roll out to a thickness for cutting about 15 dumplings. Bring large kettle of water to a boil, add 1/2 tsp. of salt. Drop dumplings into water and boil for 8 minutes.

Quick Czech Bread Dumplings

1/2 cup buttermilk baking mix
1/2 cup flour
1/4 cup milk

1 egg
1 1/2 slices bread, torn into
    small pieces

Combine all ingredients. Dough will be sticky. Roll dough in flour until it loses stickiness. Shape into a single ball and flatten slightly. In a large kettle, bring 3 quarts of water to a boil; add dumpling and bring to a boil again. Cover and boil for 16 minutes. Remove the dumpling with slotted spoon and slice into 5 to 7 slices. Recipe may be doubled as necessary, but each dumpling should be the size of a single recipe.

Noodles

2 cups flour
1 1/2 tsp. salt
1/4 tsp. baking powder
1/4 tsp. vegetable oil

3 egg yolks
1 whole egg
1/4 to 1/2 cup water

Put flour into a bowl and make a "well." Add salt, baking powder, oil, egg yolks and whole egg. Mix thoroughly. Add small amounts of water, only enough to form dough into a ball. Place dough on a well-floured cloth and knead until smooth and elastic, about 10 minutes. Cover and let rest for 10 minutes. Divide dough into 4 equal parts; roll out until paper thin. Allow to dry on tea towels for about 20 minutes. Cut into noodles as desired. Separate and let dry another 2 hours. Makes about 6 cups, or 10 ounces.

Drop Noodles for Soup

1 egg, beaten   1 cup flour

Mix egg and flour with fork until well-blended, dry and crumbly. Drop little by little into preferred boiling soup stock. These noodles take only a few minutes to cook. Excellent in chicken stock. Double ingredients for a large (8 quart) kettle of soup.

Homemade Noodles

1 1/2 cups flour   1 tsp. oil or melted shortening
2 eggs, well beaten

Put flour into small bowl; make a "well." Pour eggs and oil into well, and
mix until dough is stiff. Place dough on a floured surface; knead until
stiff. Roll out until almost paper thin. Allow to dry slightly on a clean dry
cloth, enough to prevent sticking while cutting. Cut dough into strips
about 2 inches wide; stack and cut into noodles of desired width.
Noodles may be boiled in broth, or salted water, without further drying. If
not used immediately, dry so they do not stick together, then freeze.

Noodles with Mushrooms

1 pkg. (8-oz.) fine noodles	1 lb. mushrooms
2 eggs, beaten	cooking oil
salt and pepper	light cream sauce (your choice)
	parsley

Boil noodles until tender and drain. Combine beaten eggs, salt and pepper with noodles and pour into oiled ring mold. Bake in 350° oven for 30 minutes until firm.

Sauté mushrooms in small amount of oil. Add prepared light cream sauce to mushrooms. Unmold noodle ring onto a platter and pour mushrooms into center. Garnish with sprigs of parsley.

Baked Mushrooms

large mushrooms
bread squares
butter

salt and pepper
parsley

Remove stems and wipe mushroom caps thoroughly. Cut squares of bread a little larger than mushrooms; butter squares and season with salt and pepper; sprinkle with parsley. Place mushroom caps on buttered squares of bread and heat in 350° oven for 5 minutes. Remove from oven and put a dab of butter on top of each. Return to oven and bake for an additional 15-20 minutes.

Mushrooms with Eggs

6 eggs	salt and pepper
1/4 lb. butter	paprika
2 Tbs. chopped mushrooms	hot buttered toast

Melt butter in saucepan. Add eggs, mushrooms and seasonings. Stir over medium heat until thick and creamy and eggs are cooked. Serve on hot, buttered slices of toast.

Mushrooms and Wild Rice

1 cup wild rice	1 cup sour cream
1 lb. mushrooms	salt
2 Tbs. butter	paprika

Wash wild rice thoroughly and boil in salted water, about 45 minutes. Sauté mushrooms in butter until done. Remove from heat; stir in sour cream, salt and paprika. Drain wild rice and place in a dish; make a well in the center and pour in mushrooms.

Note: Canned mushrooms labeled "broiled in butter" may be used. Heat mushrooms using liquid from the can; add cream and seasonings while heating.

Sautéed Mushrooms

mushroom caps
butter or margarine

salt and pepper
lemon juice

Wash mushroom caps; drain well or dry them in a cloth. Melt butter or margarine in a skillet, using about 1/8 lb. for each lb. of mushrooms. Put mushrooms in skillet topside down; salt and pepper evenly. When mushrooms begin to brown, turn them and cook until the liquid has evaporated, leaving only the butter or margarine. Sprinkle lemon juice over the mushrooms; serve on toast and pour remaining butter or margarine over them.

Mushroom Stuffing

(Amounts of ingredients determined by quantity desired.)

mushrooms
salt and pepper
lemon juice
cooking oil

bread crumbs
egg yolks
egg white
parsley, minced

Sauté mushrooms in cooking oil; add salt, pepper, and a few drops of lemon juice. When they are lightly cooked, chop coarsely. Use half the quantity of bread crumbs to the full quantity of mushrooms, and mix together. Add 2 egg yolks and the white of one egg (larger quantities increase egg in same proportions), and some minced parsley. Oysters may be added. Quite good for stuffing turkey.

Boiled Cabbage

1   large onion, sliced
1   head cabbage, sliced
2   Tbs. oil

3   cups water
1 1/2 cups cider vinegar
1   tsp. sugar

Sauté onion in oil. Mix with sliced cabbage. Stir together water, vinegar and sugar (and salt if desired) and add to the cabbage mixture. Cook until almost tender. Serve with potatoes and pork or ham.

Cabbage with Caraway Seed and Butter

1 med.-sized head cabbage
boiling water
1/2 tsp. salt

3/4 tsp. crushed marjoram leaves
3 Tbs. butter or margarine
1 tsp. caraway seed

Shred cabbage. Place in saucepan with 1/2 inch boiling water, salt and marjoram. Cover. Cook quickly until tender, lifting lid 3 or 4 times to allow steam to escape. Drain. Add butter, or margarine, and caraway seed. Serve hot. Serves 6.

Fried Cauliflower

1 large head cauliflower | fine dry bread crumbs
2 eggs, beaten | oil for deep-frying

Boil head of cauliflower in salted water until medium tender. Drain and carefully break into medium-sized flowerets. Dip each piece in the beaten egg, then in the bread crumbs. Fry in hot oil until golden brown. Place on absorbent paper; allow oil to drain.

Czech Sauerkraut

2 medium-sized cans sauerkraut,
   or 2 pkgs. frozen sauerkraut
1 to 2 tsp. caraway seed
1 large onion, finely chopped

lard
1 Tbs. flour (more if needed)
1 to 2 tsp. sugar (optional)

Drain sauerkraut. Wash and drain again if too sharp. Add caraway seed to taste, and enough water to cover. Cook 20-30 minutes.

   Sauté onion in small amount of lard until light brown. Add flour (and sugar if desired) and cook 5 minutes until slightly thickened. Remove from heat; add to sauerkraut and cook 5 minutes longer.

Homemade Sauerkraut

40 lbs. of fresh cabbage
scant cup of sugar

scant cup of salt
1/3 to 1/2 cup caraway seed

Remove outer leaves from cabbage, cut heads in half. Remove and save hearts. Shred cabbage with kraut cutter over large tub. Add sugar, salt and caraway seed, and mix until juicy. Pack loosely, with 1 or 2 chunks of heart, into sterilized glass jars. Add juice until about level with top. Seal tightly. Store in cool, dry place. Place jars on paper and cover top in case juice leaks during processing. Do not disturb jars while the kraut is working; allow 4 to 5 weeks. Makes about 15 quarts. Note: 10 pounds of cabbage make about 1 gallon of sauerkraut.

Sauerkraut Krisps

2 cups flour
1/2 tsp. salt
1/2 cup cold lard (shortening)
1 1/2 cups sauerkraut, drained
6 to 8 tsp. water

1 egg (optional)
milk (optional)
caraway seed (optional)
poppy seeds (optional)
salt (optional)

Combine flour and salt. Work lard, or other shortening, into flour mixture. Stir in sauerkraut. Mix well, then add water slowly until mixture forms a ball. Divide dough into 2 parts; roll out on floured surface. Roll very thin: 1/4 inch for a crisp dough, or 3/8 inch for chewy dough. Cut into strips or squares. Place on ungreased baking sheet and bake at 425° for 10-15 minutes until lightly browned. Krisp tops may be brushed with egg, or milk, and sprinkled with caraway, poppy seeds, or salt, before baking.

Potato and Mushroom Casserole

6 to 8 large potatoes, cooked and
    mashed
1/2 cup butter or margarine
1 cup milk
salt and pepper to taste
2 egg yolks, beaten

2 Tbs. chopped green onion
8 oz. fresh mushrooms, washed,
    sliced and sautéed
1/2 cup bread crumbs
2 Tbs. Parmesan cheese

To the hot, cooked and mashed potatoes, add 2 tsp. of the butter or margarine, milk, salt, pepper, beaten egg yolks and green onion. Sauté mushrooms in a small amount of butter or margarine, and add to the potato mixture. Mix together and place into a greased 2 1/2 to 3 qt. casserole dish. Melt the remaining butter and toss with the bread crumbs and Parmesan cheese. Sprinkle over the potato mixture. Bake at 325° for 25-30 minutes until hot. Serves 8.

Potato Pie

3/4 cup milk
3 eggs
3/4 tsp. salt
1/4 tsp. pepper

3 large potatoes, peeled and
   grated
3 Tbs. flour
1/4 tsp. baking powder
3 Tbs. bacon fat

Beat eggs, salt and pepper together; add milk and beat lightly. Add grated potatoes, then stir in flour and baking powder. Heat bacon fat in large, ovenproof skillet (iron is best). Pour potato mixture into skillet. Dot with butter. Bake in preheated 400° oven for 1 hour, or until golden brown. Serve with roast pork and sauerkraut.

Potato Mash

2 lbs. potatoes,
   peeled and cooked
1 cup all-purpose flour

ground poppy seed
sugar
butter, melted

Mash potatoes and flour together in a large bowl. Combine poppy seed and sugar; sprinkle generously on individual servings of potatoes. Top with melted butter.

Potato Mush

2 1/2 lbs. potatoes, peeled
  and quartered
1/2 cup butter, melted
1/2 tsp. salt

1 1/2 cups flour
1/2 cup ground poppy seed
1/2 cup sugar

Boil potatoes until tender. Drain, season with salt and mash. Shape several wells in potatoes with handle of wooden spoon. Fill wells with the flour; place over very low heat for a few minutes. Remove from heat and set aside, covered, for about 20 minutes. Then mix potato and flour to form a stiff dough. Dip a tablespoon into melted butter, and scoop potato mixture by spoonfuls onto buttered platter. Pour remaining butter over all. Sprinkle with poppy seed and sugar.

Caraway Potatoes

4 large potatoes, peeled and sliced	2 Tbs. butter
1 small onion	1 Tbs. caraway seed
hot water	1 tsp. salt

Layer potatoes and onion in a heavy kettle. Sprinkle top with caraway seed and salt. Dot with butter. Pour small amount of hot water over potatoes (just enough to see but not to cover). Bring to a boil, then simmer for 15 minutes. Serves 4.

Potato Pastry

1 cup cooked mashed potatoes (cold)	2 cups flour
1 cup butter	1 tsp. salt
	1 egg, beaten

Combine all ingredients and work into a fairly stiff dough (use more or less flour as needed). Chill for at least 1 hour, then roll out 1/4-inch thick. Cut into desired size; brush tops with beaten egg and bake at 450° for 25 minutes.

Caraway Sticks: Sprinkle potato pastry with coarse salt and caraway seed before baking.

Foamy Wine Sauce

1 cup white wine (Sauterne or
    Rhine)
4 eggs

1/2 cup sugar
2 Tbs. lemon juice

Mix all ingredients in the top of double boiler. Beat over boiling water until foamy and thick. Do not let boil (it will curdle). Serve at once as a dessert sauce over cakes or puddings.

Dandelion Wine

1 gallon dandelion blossoms
1 gallon water
2 lemons, sliced

2 oranges, sliced
5 cups sugar
1/2 cake yeast

Boil dandelion blossoms in water until liquor is fragrant. Strain. Add lemons and oranges to strained hot liquid. Add sugar and set aside to cool. When mixture is cold, add 1/2 cake yeast to each gallon of liquid.

Let stand for 1 week. Remove lemons and oranges on the second or third day. After another week, pour wine into open jugs. Put loose cover, such as towel or paper, over jugs. Allow the air to circulate. Cork jugs after 2 or 3 days.

Spiced Wine

1/2 lb. sugar
2 bottles red wine
1 lemon peel, grated

1 stick cinnamon (small)
cloves (several)

Pour wine into kettle, preferably porcelain; add half pound of sugar, grated lemon peel, cinnamon and several cloves. Place on low heat and let stand long enough for flavors to mix. Do not boil. Strain before storing or serving.

Tarts

PASTRY:
1/3 cup butter
2 egg yolks
1 cup flour
2 tsp. sugar

FILLING:
2 egg whites
3/4 cup powdered sugar
1 Tbs. currant jelly
1 Tbs. lemon juice

PASTRY: Cream butter; beat in egg yolks and sugar. Add flour and knead lightly until smooth dough is formed. Use small amounts of dough and roll out individual pieces to desired thickness (1/8 to 1/4 inch) and
contd.

press into tart forms to the rim. Bake at 350° until rosy. While still warm, tap gently to remove pastry from forms. Can be stored and used as needed.

FILLING: Beat all ingredients together until firm. Use immediately. Fruits such as strawberries or pitted cherries can be placed on tops.

Chocolate Torte

6 eggs, separated
3/4 cup sugar
1/3 cup cocoa
1 cup sifted flour

1 tsp. vanilla
1 2/3 cups powdered sugar
1 to 2 Tbs. cocoa
1/4 to 1/2 cup butter
chocolate icing

Beat egg yolks with half the sugar until thick. Beat egg whites until stiff but not dry and gradually add other half of sugar. Continue beating until sugar is incorporated. Combine egg mixtures. Sift flour and cocoa together and fold carefully into egg mixture. Fold in vanilla last. Bake in ungreased springform pan at 350° for 45 minutes. *contd.*

When cool, split into halves, top and bottom. Blend powdered sugar, cocoa and butter until creamy. Spread creamed mixture between halves. Ice top and sides with your favorite chocolate icing.

Grape Torte

1/2 cup butter
1 Tbs. sugar
2 egg yolks
1 1/2 cups sifted flour
1 tsp. salt

3 egg whites
1/2 cup powdered sugar
1/2 cup ground nuts
1 lb. seedless grapes
whipping cream

Cream butter; add sugar and egg yolks and beat until fluffy. Work in mixture of flour and salt to form a dough. Line an ungreased deep pie plate or springform cake pan with dough. Bake at 450° for 15 minutes. Allow to cool.

contd.

Beat egg whites until stiff but not dry. Gradually add powdered sugar and beat until very thick. Fold in nuts carefully. Spread this egg mixture into the baked shell and cover top with grapes. Bake at 250° for 25 minutes. Cool. Serve with whipped cream on top.

Nut and Date Torte

6 eggs, separated
1 cup powdered sugar

1 cup chopped dates
1 cup ground filberts
1 pint whipping cream

Beat egg yolks with 1/2 cup powdered sugar until thick. Beat egg whites until stiff, then slowly add 1/2 cup powdered sugar. Continue beating until stiff but not dry. Fold together both egg mixtures and carefully fold in dates and nuts. Bake in an ungreased springform pan at 300° for 45 minutes. Allow to cool in the pan. When cool, remove carefully and split to make top and bottom halves. Spread whipped cream between halves and on top to serve.

Bishop's Bread

3 eggs
1/2 cup sugar
1 tsp. lemon rind
1/2 cup chopped raisins or dates

1/2 cup chopped figs
1/2 tsp. anise seed
1 cup flour

Beat eggs until light and foamy; add sugar and continue beating until thick. Mix in lemon rind, fruit and flavoring. Add flour last, folding in carefully. Pour into greased loaf pan and bake at 350° for 45 minutes.

God's Favors

2 eggs, slightly beaten
2 Tbs. cream (sweet or sour)
2 Tbs. rum or full-bodied wine

2 cups flour
1 tsp. salt
fat for deep-frying
powdered sugar

Mix eggs with cream and rum; add to flour mixed with salt. Stir until dough is formed. Turn onto floured board and knead until smooth. Roll out thin (as for noodles); cut into diamond shapes, 3x3 inches. Cut two 1-inch slits in the middle of each piece and fry in deep fat, turning if necessary, until golden brown. Remove and place on absorbent paper. Sprinkle with powdered sugar while warm.

Christmas Cake

4 cups flour
1 Tbs. salt
1/2 cup sugar
1/2 cup butter
1 egg
1 cup warm milk
1 pkg. dry yeast, raised
   in 1/4 cup warm water

1 Tbs. grated lemon rind
1 tsp. vanilla
1/4 cup blanched
   almonds, slivered
1/2 cup seedless raisins
small amount of egg and
   milk for brushing top

Mix flour, salt and sugar. Cut butter into dry mixture. In a separate bowl, add slightly beaten egg to warm milk; stir in raised yeast. Gently stir in lemon rind and vanilla.

contd.

Turn dough onto floured board and work liquid in, kneading for about 10 minutes. Place dough in bowl and cover with cloth; let rise until doubled. Return to floured board and knead in almonds and raisins. Divide dough into 9 parts; roll each piece by hand into strips 20 inches long. Form the cake on a greased baking sheet. Twist strips together to make 3 layers of twists: the bottom one of 4 strips, middle one of 3, and the top one of 2. Stretch and twist the strips so that they sit firmly on top of each other, if necessary secure with toothpicks. Let cake rise again, then brush with mixture of equal parts egg and milk. Bake at 350° for 45 minutes or until done. Allow to rest for several hours before cutting.

Fruit Cake

1/2 cup sugar
1 egg
2 Tbs. melted butter
2 Tbs. strong black coffee
1/2 cup milk
1 tsp. baking soda
2 cups flour

1/2 cup chopped walnuts
1 Tbs. each: chopped
    candied orange peel,
    citron peel, cherries
1/2 tsp. each: cinnamon,
    cloves, allspice

Beat sugar with egg; add melted butter, coffee, milk and baking soda. Combine flour, nuts, chopped fruits and spices. Add to liquids; mix well. Bake in greased loaf tin at 350° for about 40 minutes. Allow to rest for several hours before cutting.

Poppy Seed Cake

1/3 cup poppy seeds
1 cup buttermilk
1 cup margarine
1 1/2 cups sugar
4 eggs
1 orange rind, grated
1/2 tsp. vanilla

1/2 tsp. salt
2 1/2 cups sifted flour
2 tsp. baking powder
1 tsp. soda
2 Tbs. granulated sugar and
   2 tsp. cinnamon, mixed

Soak poppy seeds in buttermilk overnight. Cream margarine and sugar until smooth. Beat in eggs one at a time. Stir in grated orange rind, vanilla and salt. Sift flour, baking powder and soda together. Add flour

contd.

mixture and poppy seed-buttermilk mixture alternately to the creamed mixture. Mix until smooth. Pour half of batter into a greased and floured 10-inch tube pan or fluted ring mold. Sprinkle sugar and cinnamon mixture on this half of batter, then add rest of batter. Bake at 350° for 35 minutes, or until toothpick inserted comes out clean.

Poppy Seed Coffee Cake

2 eggs
1/4 cup sugar
1/4 cup butter, softened
1 tsp. salt
3/4 cup warm milk

3 cups flour
1 pkg. dry yeast, raised
1/2 tsp. mace or vanilla
poppy seed filling

Beat eggs with sugar. Add softened butter, salt, milk, 1 cup flour, mace or vanilla, and beat again. Add raised yeast; mix well. Turn dough onto floured board and stir in remaining flour, kneading the dough until smooth and not sticky. Roll into a rectangular sheet, 1/2-inch thick. Spread poppy seed filling (see *Fillings*) on dough, roll up and put in a well-greased fluted cake form. Let rise until almost double. Bake at 350° for about 45 minutes.

Poppy Seed Strudel

2 cups flour	1 Tbs. sugar
1/2 cup butter	1 pkg. dry yeast, raised
2 egg yolks	1/2 tsp. salt
1/2 cup warm milk	1 egg, beaten
	poppy seed filling *(Fillings)*

Work butter into flour. Mix egg yolks with milk, add sugar, raised yeast and salt; add to flour and butter mixture and work until smooth. Turn dough onto floured work surface and knead lightly. Roll out into 1/3-inch thickness; spread with poppy seed filling (see *Fillings*). Roll into a strudel and place on a greased baking sheet. Cover with cloth and let rise until double. Brush top with beaten egg and bake at 350° for about 45 minutes.

Kolaches

1/4 cup lukewarm water
2 pkgs. dry yeast
1 Tbs. sugar
1 cup butter or margarine
2 cups milk
4 egg yolks

2 whole eggs
1/2 cup sugar
1/2 tsp. mace
1/2 tsp. grated lemon rind
1 1/2 tsp. salt
6 to 7 cups flour
melted butter for brushing

Dissolve yeast in lukewarm water, add 1 Tbs. sugar and let set until bubbly. Melt butter and add 2 cups milk; heat until warm. Beat yolks

contd.

and whole eggs together; add 1/2 cup sugar and continue beating until thick. Add warm milk/butter liquid. Stir together with yeast, mace, salt and lemon rind. Beat in flour, preferably with a wooden spoon, 1 cup at a time. When dough becomes too thick to beat with spoon, turn onto floured board and knead until smooth and silky. Put kneaded dough into a greased bowl and let rise in warm place until doubled. Place dough on lightly floured board and divide into 6 large pieces. Cut each of these into 12 smaller pieces. Shape into walnut-sized balls by rolling dough with hand. Place on greased baking sheet 2 inches apart and brush each ball with melted butter. Let rise until almost double in size. Press indent in center and fill with filling (see *Fillings*). Let rise again until they appear light. Bake at 400° for 7 to 10 minutes. Brush warm kolaches with butter. Makes 6 dozen. (Toppings and fillings on pages 101-108.)

Crumb Topping for Kolaches

1/2 cup sugar
1 cup flour
1/4 cup butter or margarine

1/4 tsp. cinnamon
1/4 tsp. salt (omit if using
    margarine)

Combine all ingredients, working with a pastry blender until crumbly. Use as a topping for kolaches or coffee cakes.

Butter Rum Filling

1/2 cup powdered sugar	1 egg yolk
1/2 cup softened sweet butter	1 Tbs. rum

Cream butter and powdered sugar together. Add rest of ingredients and beat until light and fluffy. Enough for about 1 dozen kolaches.

Cabbage Filling

1/2 cup butter or margarine
4 cups finely chopped cabbage
2 Tbs. sugar

1 tsp. salt
1/8 tsp. pepper
1/8 tsp. allspice

Melt butter in a heavy saucepan; add cabbage, salt, pepper and sugar. Cook over medium heat for about 30 minutes, until cabbage is soft and lightly browned. Stir constantly while cooking. Mix in allspice last. Enough for 3 dozen kolaches.

Cherry Filling

6 Tbs. cornstarch
1 cup sugar
1/4 tsp. salt
2 cans sour red cherries

1 tsp. red food coloring
1 tsp. vanilla
1/2 tsp. almond flavoring

Mix sugar, cornstarch and salt. Drain cherries and add juice to sugar mixture; cook and stir until thick. Stir in remaining ingredients. Enough filling for 3 dozen kolaches.

Honey-Poppy Seed Filling

1 cup ground poppy seed
1/2 cup milk
2 Tbs. sugar

1 Tbs. honey
1 tsp. allspice

Bring poppy seed and milk to a slow boil and simmer for about 5 minutes.
Stir constantly until thick. Add sugar and honey and cook another 2
minutes. Add allspice last. Enough for 3 dozen kolaches.

Nut Butter Filling

1/2 cup powdered sugar
1/2 cup softened sweet butter
1/4 cup grated walnuts

1 Tbs. rum
1/2 tsp. vanilla

Cream sugar and butter together. Add rest of ingredients and beat until light and fluffy. Enough for about 1 dozen kolaches.

Poppy Seed Filling

1/2 lb. ground poppy seed
1 cup water
1 cup milk
1 Tbs. butter or margarine
1 tsp. vanilla

1/2 tsp. cinnamon
1 cup sugar
1/2 cup crushed graham
    crackers
1/2 cup softened raisins

Boil poppy seed in 1 cup water until thickened; add milk and boil slowly for about 10 minutes (be careful that it does not scorch). Add butter, vanilla and cinnamon, then sugar; continue cooking for about 5 minutes. Remove from heat and add graham cracker crumbs and raisins. Enough to fill 3 dozen kolaches.

Prune Filling

1 lb. pitted dry prunes, cooked
1 cup liquid from cooked prunes
1/2 cup sugar

1 Tbs. lemon juice
1 tsp. grated lemon rind
1/2 tsp. cinnamon

Cover prunes with cold water; stir in sugar, and bring to a boil. Reduce heat and cook slowly, stirring constantly until smooth and thick. Remove from heat and add lemon juice, grated rind and cinnamon. Apricots may be used in place of prunes. Enough for 3 dozen kolaches.

Christmas Recipes from Czechoslovakia

The following eleven recipes are from a wonderful collection in their old, original form of more than a half-century ago. "As written" they will warm heart and hearth, and add flavor to your holiday eve. If you wish to update them, use the NOTES pages following the recipes.

Fancy Almond Cookies

Christmas Recipes from Czechoslovakia

1 cup sugar
1/2 cup blanched almonds, cut
    into narrow slivers

4 egg whites
1 Tbs. sugar
1/2 tsp. vanilla

Mix 1 cup sugar and almonds and set aside. Beat egg whites with 1 Tbs. sugar until stiff (so it could be cut). Add sugar and almond mixture to egg whites. Fold in vanilla, easily. Place on tin waxed with beeswax. Make hole in center of mixture to form rings. Bake in slow (300°) oven 'til light brown. Note: Do not remove from the oven at once, but turn off the oven, open the door and leave for about 5 minutes. Cool gradually, away from a draft.

Nut Cake

Christmas Recipes from Czechoslovakia

1 lb. ground nutmeats (hazel nuts
    preferred)
2 1/2 cups sugar
11 egg yolks
peel from 1 lemon
5 egg whites

Frost with:
1 cup powdered sugar
1 cup butter
2 egg yolks
2 Tbs. strong coffee

Mix ground nutmeats and sugar. Add egg yolks one at a time, rub 'til light. Add grated lemon rind. Beat egg whites 'til stiff. Fold into nutmeat mixture. Bake in 2 pans, greased and floured, in mild oven (300°) for 3/4 hour.

FROSTING: Cream powdered sugar, butter, egg yolks and coffee for about 1/2 hour. Whipped cream or plain butter filling can be used between layers.

Yolk Cookies

Christmas Recipes from Czechoslovakia

6 eggs, hard-boiled
1 cup butter
1 cup sugar
3 egg yolks
1 whole egg

grated lemon peel
pinch of ground mace
3 Tbs. milk
1 egg yolk, lightly beaten
almonds, chopped

Boil 6 eggs for 20 minutes. Let cool in cold water; peel and separate yolks. Cream butter, sugar, 3 egg yolks and 1 whole egg; add grated lemon peel and pinch of mace to flavor, and mix well. Add cold hard-boiled egg yolks and mix until smooth. Stir in milk. Roll out on floured board; cut with cookie cutter. Brush with raw egg yolk and sprinkle with chopped almonds. Bake in moderate (350°) oven until lightly browned.

Ladyfingers

Christmas Recipes from Czechoslovakia

8 egg yolks
1/2 lb. sugar

8 egg whites
2 cups sifted flour
powdered sugar

Beat egg yolks and sugar till light and foamy. Beat egg whites until stiff, then add to yolk mixture. Add sifted flour, and stir until smooth. Pour batter into floured finger molds or on waxed paper pressed into finger forms. Bake in slow (300°) oven. Dust with powdered sugar.

Almond Ladyfingers

Christmas Recipes from Czechoslovakia

1/4 lb. almonds, blanched and
    chopped very fine
14 eggs
10 Tbs. sugar

2 Tbs. sifted flour
powdered sugar

Separate egg whites and yolks; divide whites into 2 and 7 (put remaining aside). Mix almonds with 2 egg whites and add the 10 Tbs. granulated sugar. Mix well. Add 14 egg yolks and mix for about 1/2 hour. Whip 7 egg whites and add to the almond and yolk mixture. Stir in sifted flour. Spoon batter into floured finger forms. Bake in slow (300°) oven until light and golden. Powder with powdered sugar when done.

Sugar Cookies

Christmas Recipes from Czechoslovakia

1 cup sugar	3 1/2 cups flour
1/2 cup butter	2 eggs
1/2 cup lard	pinch of salt
1/2 cup buttermilk	1 tsp. vanilla or grated rind
1 heaping tsp. baking powder	of orange or lemon

Cream sugar, butter and lard. Dissolve baking powder in buttermilk; add to creamed mixture. Stir in flour, eggs, salt and flavoring. Roll out thin on lightly floured board and sprinkle generously with sugar. Cut the cookies into different shapes with cookie cutters. Bake in 350° oven until slightly colored.

Chocolate Pecan Cookies

Christmas Recipes from Czechoslovakia

1 cup sugar
1 egg
2 squares melted chocolate
1/4 cup butter

1/2 cup flour
1 tsp. vanilla
1 cup chopped pecans

Mix all ingredients until smooth. With a teaspoon make little heaps (as a walnut) on a floured and greased tin sheet. Bake in slow oven (300°) about 6 to 8 minutes. You can also place 1/2 a nut on each cookie while still warm. Makes 3 dozen.

Almond Rolls

Christmas Recipes from Czechoslovakia

1 cup butter
3 Tbs. powdered sugar (heaping)
1 tsp. vanilla

2 egg yolks
1 cup almonds, blanched
   and ground
2 cups sifted flour

Work all ingredients together. Roll into a long oval roll and cut into pieces 3/8 inch thick. Roll each piece and shape into a crescent. Place on lightly greased tin sheet. Bake in moderate oven (350°) until pinkish brown. Carefully remove from tin sheet and roll in additional powdered sugar.

Nut Rolls

Christmas Recipes from Czechoslovakia

DOUGH:
1/2 cup milk
1/2 tsp. sugar
1 1/2 cakes Fleischmann's yeast
3/4 lb. butter
2 Tbs. sugar
1 lb. flour
6 egg yolks

FILLING:
1/2 lb. English walnuts
1 cup sugar
1 heaping Tbs. butter
2 egg yolks
6 ground vanilla cookies
2 egg whites
powdered sugar for
    sprinkling

Heat the milk until lukewarm; mix with the yeast and 1/2 tsp. of sugar, then set aside to rise. *contd.*

Put the flour, butter and 2 tbs. of sugar on a breadboard and cut with a knife until it appears like cornmeal. Make a circle of this flour mixture and pour the egg yolks and the fermented yeast into center. Mix well with a knife, knead the dough, and place in a bowl. Cover the bowl and allow it to set overnight in a cool place (or in a refrigerator for two hours).

Roll the dough to a 1/4-inch thickness and cut into 4-inch squares. Spread the filling on the squares and roll the dough diagonally over the filling. Place the rolls on a greased shallow pan (about 1/2 inch apart) and allow them to rise 10 minutes in a warm place. Brush with a beaten egg and bake for 10 minutes at 450° (5 minutes in the bottom of the oven and 5 minutes in the top of the oven). Sprinkle with powdered sugar. (This recipe makes 5 dozen.)

FILLING: Roll nuts with a rolling pin until very fine. Mix nuts, sugar, egg yolks and cookies well. Then add two beaten egg whites and mix well. Fill the rolls.

Christmas Cherries

Christmas Recipes from Czechoslovakia

1/2 cup shortening
1/4 cup sugar
1 egg yolk
1/2 tsp. vanilla
1 tsp. grated orange rind

1 1/2 tsp. grated lemon rind
1 tsp. lemon juice
1 egg white, beaten slightly
15 candied cherries
1/2 cup chopped nuts

Cream butter and sugar. Add egg yolk, vanilla, grated rinds, juice and flour. Mix well and chill. Roll into balls. Dip in egg white and then roll in nuts. Make an impression with finger in each ball and place 1/2 a cherry in each cookie. Bake in 350° oven for 20 minutes.

Anise Shells

Weigh two eggs, use same weight of sugar, half the weight of flour. Use as many eggs as you wish. Separate eggs. Beat yolks until lemon colored, add sugar gradually and beat. Add flour, pinch of salt and beaten whites of eggs.

Wax your cookie tins. Wipe surplus wax off with paper towel. (This must be beeswax, not paraffin.) Drop by spoonfuls on the tin. Sprinkle a few grains of anise on tops. Sift powdered sugar on tops, careful not to get any on tin (use small strainer). Bake in a quick (400°) oven until golden brown. Take out of oven. Use spatula to loosen cookies and curl each cookie quickly over wooden spoon, or curl with fingers, leaning cookies one against another to help them stay curled. You must work very fast. If they get too cool to curl, warm the loosened cookies on the tin.

Food for Thought

The flavor of life is enhanced, not only at table, but through the fullness of understandiing and appreciation of a heritage. The Czechoslovakian heritage is rich in these values as demonstrated by the expression of thought contained in the maxims, proverbs and sayings attributed to Czech culture.

The Sokol Maxims declare a strength of conviction, a voice of a people. Sokol is a Czechoslovakian organization that promotes physical fitness, moral soundness, mental alertness and brotherhood.

The essence of the collection of sage observations and sayings is at times whimsical, practical, profound, priceless and always precious. They should be relished as "spice" in the life of the people to whom they relate.

Sokol Maxims and Mottos

Your soul enthused, your cheeks aglow, your arms a lion's might.

Nadšení v duši, v líci žár, lví sílu ve své paži!

Forward, forward; backward not a step.

Ku předu, ku předu; zpátky ni krok.

contd.

With a lion's might and a falcon's flight.
Siloulví, vzletem sokolím.

Develop your strength; serve your country.
Paže tuź, vlasti služ.

contd.

Your country in your soul, your strength in your willing arms, and courage in your heart.

V duši vlast, v paži sílu, v srdci smělost.

Break in twain, leap across, but never cringe or crawl.

Přelom, přeskoč, nepodlez.

contd.

The world moves where might is most applied.
Tám svět se nahne, kam síla se napře.

Liberty, equality, brotherhood.
Volnost, rovnost, bratrství.

contd.

Nor gain, nor glory.
Ni zisk, ni sláva.

Either attain or fall, either naught or all.
Buď dospět, nebo padnout, buď všecko, nebo nic.

contd.

One for all and all for one.
Jeden za všechny a všichni za jednoho.

Truth conquers.
Pravda vítězí.

Seasonings: a Dash of Sage—a Pinch of Salt

Water is the cheapest medicine.
Voda je nejlacinější lék.

What was not given you from above cannot be bought at an apothecary shop.
Komu není z hůry dáno v apatice nekoupí.

contd.

Without work, there are no kolaches.
Bez práci nejsou koláče.

A good name is the best inheritance.
Dobré jméno nejlepší dědictví.

contd.

A loving word is better than sweet kolache.

Laskavé slovo lepší než sladký koláč.

Whose bread you eat, sing his song.

Či chleb jídáš toho piseň zpíváš.

contd.

When you oversalt the goose, you will appreciate a pitcher of beer.

Když husu přesolíš, žbánek piva oželíš.

Everything has an end, but link sausage has two!

Všecko ma konec, a jaternice dvá!

contd.

Toast: Long life to the drinker!
At žije kdo pije!

Morning rain never lasts long.
Ranní déšť neni stalí.

contd.

Better a sparrow in the hand than a pigeon on the roof.

Lepši vrabec v hrsti, než holub na střeše.

Even the winner of a war suffers from lack of bread.

contd.

What was collected and saved with a teaspoon is now being thrown out with a shovel!

A handful of friends is better than a wagonful of gold.

contd.

Who goes for a day in the forest should take bread for a week.

The fish does not go after the hook, but after the bait.

contd.

Many a friend was lost through a joke, but none was ever gained so.

Winter to Spring:

After New Year's Day, every day gets longer by a chicken's step.

Po nový rok, dni jsou delši o slepičí krok.

contd.

A final truism:

"Every Czech is a musician."

From a collection of European proverbs, the musical aspect of Czechoslovakian culture is displayed in the celebration of life through music: at home with family, at festive gatherings, at public meeting places, wherever there is a song to be sung.

The lyrical refrains of "The Czechoslovak National Anthems," printed on the following pages, express this spirit of home and nation.

The Czechoslovak National Anthems

Part 1:

Czech National Anthem, *Where Is My Home?*

Where is my home, where is my home?
Streams are rushing through the meadows,
Mid the rocks sigh fragrant pine groves,
Orchards decked in Spring's array
Scenes of Paradise portray!
And this land of wondrous beauty
Is the Czech land, home of mine!
Is the Czech land, home of mine!

contd.

National Anthems contd.

Part 2:

Slovak National Anthem, *Thunder over the Tatra Mountains*

Tatra's filled with fiery lightning and with thunder.
Tatra's filled with fiery lightning and with thunder.
Brothers, let's be daring,
While ahead we're faring,
Slovaks ne'er will sunder.
Brothers, let's be daring,
While ahead we're faring,
Slovaks ne'er will sunder.

contd.

National Anthems contd.

Another translation of Part 2 is:

Lightning strikes our mighty Tatra tempest-shaken,
Lightning strikes our mighty Tatra tempest-shaken.
Stand we fast, friends of mine.
Storms must pass, sun will shine.
Slovaks shall awaken.

A National Character Defined

> "Promise me,
> Command me,
> Threaten me,
> But I will not be a traitor!
> My colors are Red and White,
> My heritage Honesty and Strength!"

This famous verse was written by Karel Havlícek (1821-1856), Czecho-slovakian statesman and patriot.

NOTES